Find Out
about Christians

by Mary Hawes

Illustrated by Julie Moores

SCRIPTURE UNION PUBLISHING

London Sydney Cape Town Philadelphia Toronto

Acknowledgements
Cover photograph
John Grayston, with thanks to
St. Mary Magdelene's Primary School, Islington

Cover design:
Tony Cantale Graphics

© Scripture Union 1986
First Published 1986
Reprinted 1987, 1989, 1991

Published in the UK by
Scripture Union, 130 City Road, London EC1V 2NJ
Published in Australia by
Anzea Publishers, PO Box 115, Flemington Markets, NSW2129
Distributed in Southern Africa by
SUPA, 83 Camp Ground Road, Rondebosh 7700
Published in USA by
Scripture Union, 7000 Ludlow Street, Upper Darby, PA 19082
Published in Canada by
Scripture Union, 300 Steelcase Road West, Unit 19, Markham, Ontario L3R 2W2

ISBN 0 86201 334 8 UK

Find Out about Christians

ISBN 0 85892 283 5 Australia

Typeset by Central Typesetting Service Limited, London.

Printed by Ebenezer Baylis and Son Limited,
The Trinity Press, Worcester and London.

Dear Parents,

We live in an exciting world. But it is also a changing world. Even the youngest members of our families can be aware of pressures and anxieties. As parents we are rightly concerned for our children's well being in every part of their lives.

Above all, we want to share with our children the security and hope we find in our relationship with Christ himself. It is our privilege to help them learn how to listen to God as he speaks to us through the Bible and to grow in a relationship with him that is right for every stage in their development.

We in Scripture Union hope that these four Find Out books will give you a special way of helping your children in these important ways. The books are for you and your children to share together, so:

● Try to find a regular time when your child can be sure that she or he has your undivided attention.

● Focus on the *value* of the time you spend together, not its length. Ten minutes may well be long enough. So prepare yourself to be relaxed and unhurried for that time!

● Make it a high point in the day which you will look forward to together.

● Use the Good News version of the Bible. Some of the puzzles may not work with other versions.

● Work through the 'About the Bible' pages together to help your child learn how to use the Bible.

● Each day, help your child to find the Bible verses for him or herself. Read them aloud together, take turns at reading or encourage your child to read them aloud to you.

● Have a pencil and some crayons or coloured pencils ready to use.

● Be ready to listen to your child. Encourage your child to put his or her ideas into their own words, but don't press for 'right' answers.

● The 'Prayer time' everyday will give you ideas and prayers. To start with, you may like to pray the words for your child. Or you might start the prayer and leave a gap for your child to add words or sentences of their own. Gently encouraging a step by step response will bring great rewards.

We hope that the Find Out times you share together with God will bring you special enjoyment and strength.

Mary Hawes

'Find Out' Editor

A prayer for parents

'Heavenly Father, thank you for the gift of life. But thank you even more for the new life you give to our family through your Son Jesus Christ. May we have the help of your Holy Spirit to walk together with Jesus as our Way, to be strong together with him as our Truth and to be joyful together with him as our Life. Amen.'

'. . . I am sure that he (God) is able to keep safe until that Day what he has entrusted to me.'
2 Timothy 1.12

About the Bible

There are millions of books in the world. But the Bible is *special*. It is different from every other book.

What does your Bible look like? Draw it here.

● The Bible tells us about God.
● The Bible tells us about people – and the way God wants people to live.
● The Bible shows us how we can get to know God. It tells us how we can become God's friends.

God speaks to us as we read the Bible.

Prayer time

Lord God, I want to read the Bible and find out about you. Please help me to understand what I read. Amen.

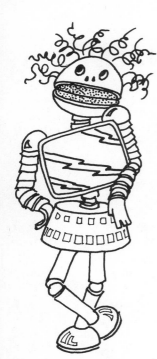

Meet Polly Puter and Sam Sharp. They will help you find out about God as you read your Bible.

Each day there is a 'Find out' verse to read. Polly will tell you where to find it in your Bible.

This tells you which Bible book to find. *(The contents list at the front of your Bible will tell you which page it begins on.)*

This number tells you which chapter to read.

This number tells you which verse to read.

Can you find these 'Find out' verses? Write their page numbers here.

Isaiah 6:3

Psalm 96:4

(Get your mum or dad to help you if you get stuck.)

Don't forget

When you use 'Find out' you will need:

a Good News Bible
a pen or pencil
some crayons

Find out about Christians

Contents

All sorts of people

**Two fishermen:
Simon Peter and
Andrew**

Matthew
4:18,19

These fact-files belong to two of the
first Christians. Polly's 'Find out'
verses will help you fill them in.

Join the dots to finish
drawing their 'photos'.

Name Simon Peter

Job ....

Where did he meet Jesus?

....

Name ....

Job ....

Where did he meet Jesus?

....

Simon Peter and Andrew were
ordinary people. But Jesus chose
them to become his special friends.

Prayer time

Lord Jesus, thank you that
ordinary people can become
your special friends. Amen.

Use these face shapes to draw some of your friends.

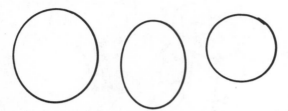

This is Zacchaeus. He didn't have any friends. People didn't like him because he was a tax collector and cheated people.

Read Polly's 'Find out' verse to see what Jesus said to Zacchaeus.

Zacchaeus was so surprised! Jesus wanted to be his friend. No one had ever done that before!

One day Zacchaeus heard that Jesus was coming to his town. He climbed a tree to get a good look at Jesus.

Turn the page upside down to see how Zacchaeus felt now.

Jesus wants everyone to become his friend – even people that nobody else likes!

Prayer time

Thank Jesus for your friends.

Luke 10:38, 39

Peter likes visiting his Aunty Carol. She lets him help her make pastry people.

Jesus had some friends that he liked visiting. They were two sisters called Mary and Martha.

Read Polly's 'Find out' verses and work out which one is which.

Can you find the way to Mary and Martha's house?

start here

Prayer time

Lord Jesus, thank you for ....
(Think of someone you like visiting.)
I like going to their house. Amen.

DAY 4

All sorts of people
An angry man:
Saul – part one

Acts 8:3

Alex borrowed Sharon's favourite jigsaw. When he gave it back, some of the pieces were missing.

Some of it's missing! I hate you.

JIGSAW PUZZLE

Have you felt like that?

Polly's 'Find out' verse tells us about a man who said 'I hate you' to Christians.
What was his name?

Write down the first letter of each object.

He hated the Christians because they loved Jesus. They kept telling everyone that Jesus was alive. Saul hated them so much that he didn't care what happened to them.

It was very frightening to be a Christian when Saul was around.

Prayer time

There are still some places in the world where people hate Christians. Ask God to look after the Christians in those places.

DAY 5

All sorts of people
An angry man:
Saul – part two

Acts
9:3-6

Damascus

Saul set off for Damascus. He wanted to find the Christians who lived there. 'I will punish them for saying that Jesus is alive', he said, 'Jesus is NOT alive. He is dead'.

But on his way to Damascus, something very strange happened. Read what it was in Polly's 'Find out' verses.

Damascus

When Saul got up, he couldn't see anything. He had to be led into Damascus.

But Saul was beginning to find out that he had been wrong about Jesus. Jesus WAS alive after all!

Prayer time

Does your family know someone who doesn't believe in Jesus? Put their name in this prayer.

Lord Jesus, please help

....

to know that you really are alive. Amen.

Acts 9:17

Ananias lived in Damascus. He loved Jesus very much.

One day, Jesus said to him, 'Ananias, Saul is in Damascus. I want you to visit him.'

How do you think Ananias felt?

pleased

cross

sad

frightened

excited

But because Ananias loved Jesus, he went to visit Saul. Polly's 'Find out' verse will tell you what Ananias said.

Suddenly, Saul could see again! But that wasn't the only change. Saul stopped hating Christians.

Jesus changed Saul from his enemy into one of his best friends.

Prayer time

Thank you, Lord, that you can change unkind and cruel people into kind, caring people who love you. Amen.

A game to make.

1 Cut ten face shapes out of the cardboard.

2 Draw ladies' faces on three of the shapes, and men's faces on the rest.

3 On the back of each face, write a name.
Ladies' names: *Mary, Martha, Lydia*
Men's names: *Zacchaeus, Saul, Simon, Peter, Andrew, Dr Luke, Crispus, Timothy*

4 Attach a paper clip to each face and put them into the shoebox.

5 Attach the magnet to one end of the string (ask your mum or dad to help you).

6 Tie the other end of the string to the pencil.

7 Without looking, dip the magnet into the shoebox and try to catch a face.

8 Count how many letters there are in the face's name to find out your score.

All sorts of people
A rich lady: Lydia

Acts 16:14,15

When Saul became a Christian, he changed completely. He wanted everyone to know about Jesus. He had a new Christian name, Paul, to show how different he was.

One day, Paul and his friends went down to a riverside. They met some women there who loved God. The women used to meet there often. They sang songs to God and they prayed to him.

One of the women was called Lydia. When Paul told her the Good News that Jesus is God's Son, she became a Christian.

Read Polly's 'Find out' verses, and tick what Lydia's job was.

☐ She sold fruit and vegetables.

☐ She made tents.

☐ She sold purple cloth.

Prayer time

Thank you, Lord, for ....
....
who tells me about you. Amen.

DAY 8
All sorts of people
A prison officer

Acts 16:30

Can you guess where Paul and his friend Silas are?

They were in jail because they had been telling people about Jesus. But even being in jail couldn't stop Paul singing and praising the Lord Jesus.

Suddenly there was an earthquake! All the prison doors flew open. The jailer thought that the prisoners would all run away.

But Paul called out, 'Don't worry. We're all here.'

Read Polly's 'Find out' verse and work out what the jailer said.

Sir, what must
_ _ _ _
_ _ _ _
_ _ _ _ _ ?

Paul was able to tell him the Good News about Jesus, and he and his family all became Christians.

Prayer time

Think of a chorus which says how great Jesus is and sing it for him now.

Doctor, doctor I feel like a dustbin.

Don't talk rubbish!

Do you know any more doctor jokes?

Doctors are important people. They look after us when we are ill. They know about the best medicines to give us.

Dr Luke was a writer, as well as a doctor. One of his books was called 'The Acts of the Apostles'. Can you find out which other book he wrote?

It's near the beginning of the New Testament.

Polly's 'Find out' verse tells us that one of the first Christians was a doctor.

Prayer time

Put your doctor's name in this prayer.

Father God, thank you for

Doctor .... Please help him/her to take good care of people who aren't well. Amen.

All sorts of people
A church leader: Crispus

Acts 18:8

Meet Crispus and his family. Polly's 'Find out' verse will tell you where they lived.

Where do you go to meet other Christians and worship God? Draw a picture of it here.

Write down the first letter of each object.

Crispus was an important person. He was in charge of the synagogue. The synagogue is the place where Jewish people meet to worship God.

When Crispus became a Christian, he was able to tell the people about God – and about God's Son, Jesus, too!

Prayer time

Thank God for your church leader.

DAY 11

All sorts of people
A young man: Timothy

Acts 16:1

This is Timothy and his family. When Timothy was small, his mother used to teach him about God. She told him stories about people who obeyed God a long time ago.

Get Timothy to his house. (Polly's 'Find out' verse will help you find the way.)

Rome

Corinth

Lystra

The stories helped Timothy to learn about God and the things he does. As Timothy grew up, he remembered all that his mother had taught him about God. Later, he became one of God's helpers, and helped people learn about God's Son, Jesus.

Prayer time

Father God, thank you for all the stories in the Bible which help me learn about you. Amen.

The first Christians . . .

. . . **loved Jesus very much**

John 12:3

Joseph wanted to show his gran how much he loved her. So he gave her a present.

Join the dots to see what the present was.

How did Mary show Jesus that she loved him? Read Polly's 'Find out' verse.

Some people thought it was an odd thing to do. But Jesus knew it was Mary's way of showing that she loved him.

Think of a way you could show Jesus that you love him. Ask your mum or dad to give you some ideas.

She poured _ _ _ _ _ _ _ _ over

Jesus's _ _ _ _ and wiped them

with her _ _ _ _.

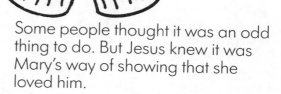

Prayer time

Lord Jesus, help me to show that I love you by doing things that will please you. Amen.

DAY 13

The first Christians . . .

. . . wanted to live Jesus's way

John 14:23

Have you ever played 'Simon says'? One person is 'Simon' and everyone else does what Simon tells them to.

Read Polly's 'Find out' verse and work out what Jesus said.

Go by the sounds.

If U ... g bm U obey bm.

As you read your Bible with 'Find out', you'll discover some of the things Jesus wants you to do.

It's a good game to play.

Christians want to do the things that Jesus tells them to. But they aren't playing a game. They obey Jesus because they love him and want to live his way.

Prayer time

Lord Jesus, please help me to obey you so that I will live the way you want me to. Amen.

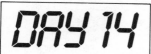 **DAY 14**

The first Christians . . .
. . . loved God and obeyed him

1 John 5:3

Mum wasn't very well. She had to stay in bed. Alan and John did as much as they could to help her.

What jobs did Alan and John do?

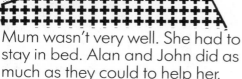

Read Polly's 'Find out' verse.

Christians show that they love God by obeying his commands. That means they try to do the things God asks them to.

Where do we find God's commands?

Use a mirror.

ɘldiꓭ ɘʜɟ nI.

Alan and John showed that they loved Mum by doing the things she asked them to.

Prayer time

Lord God, please help me to show that I love you. Help me to do the things you ask me to. Amen.

DAY 15

The first Christians . . .
. . . wanted everyone to know about Jesus

Acts 14:21

Sarah was very excited. The Queen was visiting her school, and Sarah was going to give her some flowers. Sarah told everyone about her good news.

I'm going to meet the Queen.

Read Polly's 'Find out' verse.

Paul and Barnabas had some Good News which they wanted to tell everyone.

Colour the shapes with a dot in to show who the Good News was all about.

They wanted everyone to know that Jesus was alive!

Prayer time

Who could you tell about Jesus? Put their name in this prayer.
Dear Lord, please help me to tell

....

about you. Amen.

The first Christians . . .
. . . talked to God

Who have you talked to today?

Mum ☐

Dad ☐

Sister ☐

We spend a lot of time talking. We tell people what we've been doing. We ask people to help us. We tell people how we are feeling.

Brother ☐

It's important to talk to people. And it's important to talk to God.

Teacher ☐

Read Polly's 'Find out' verse. The first Christians talked to God about everything that happened to them.

Pet dog/cat ☐

We'll learn more about talking to God later in this book.

Friends ☐

Prayer time

Lord God, I'm glad I can talk to you. It's fun! Amen.

Anyone else? ....

The first Christians . . .
. . . helped each other

I Corinthians 16 : 1,2

Have you ever needed some help?
Write or draw about it here.

The first Christians in Jerusalem
needed help.

Read Polly's 'Find out' verses to find
out how the Christians in Corinth
were going to help them.

☐ By sending them food.
☐ By sending money.
☐ By writing a letter.
☐ By buying a house.

The Christians in Corinth were glad
that they could help the Christians in
Jerusalem.

Jesus still wants Christians to help
each other. Talk about the way the
people in your church do that.

Prayer time

Tell Jesus about the way the
people in your church are helping
other Christians.

DAY 18

The first Christians . . .
. . . **shared things**

Acts 2:44

Oh no! Where are my sandwiches?

Barry forgot to take his lunch to school.

The first Christians knew that Jesus wanted them to help other people. One way they could do that was by sharing their things.

Use a mirror to see how Maria helped Barry.

crisps

Maria

Read Polly's 'Find out' verse.

Talk to your mum or dad about how you could share the things you have.

She shared her sandwiches and crisps.

Prayer time

Dear Jesus, please help me to share the things I have with other people. Amen.

DAY 19

The first Christians . . .
. . . had meals together

Acts 2:46

Mum, can I go to Philip's house for tea?

Peter likes going to Philip's house for tea. Sometimes, if the weather's nice, they have a picnic outside.

It's fun to have your meals with other people.
Polly's 'Find out' verse tells us that the first Christians enjoyed having meals together.

Sing this prayer to the tune of 'Ten green bottles'. You could use it to say thank you for your meals.

Prayer time

Thank you, Father, for all good things you give,
Thank you, Father, for all I need to live,
Help me share with others
Help everyone to see
I want to thank you, Father, for always loving me.

Make some biscuits to share with your family.

You will need:
125g soft margarine
125g caster sugar
1 egg, lightly beaten
250g plain flour
¼ teaspoonful mixed spice

1 Put the margarine and sugar in a big bowl. Cream them together with a wooden spoon.

2 Beat the egg into the creamed mixture.

3 Sieve the flour and spice into the mixture a little at a time. Mix it together until it is smooth.

4 Roll out the mixture on a floured board.

5 Cut out shapes and put them on a greased baking tray.

6 Bake them in the oven (180°C, 350°F, Gas Mark 4) for 8-10 minutes until they are golden.

7 Cool them on a wire tray.

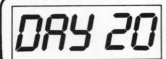

DAY 20

The first Christians . . .
Many people became Christians

Acts 6:7

Have you heard about Jesus?

The first Christians couldn't stop talking about Jesus. They wanted everyone to know that he was God's Son.

Polly's 'Find out' verse says that more and more people heard about Jesus and became Christians.

Here is a picture of some of them. Make it 'grow' by either drawing more people or cutting out pictures of people and sticking them on.

Prayer time

Lord Jesus, lots of people have heard the Good News about you and become Christians. I'm glad about that. Please may lots more people hear about you. Amen.

DAY 21

The first Christians...
But not everyone liked them

Acts 5:17,18

Tim is jealous of Kelvin because Kelvin has lots of friends.

So Tim started to tell lies about Kelvin.

I saw Kelvin take some sweets out of your bag.

When we are jealous it can make us do things that hurt other people.

The High Priest and his friends were jealous when they saw all the wonderful things that God was doing with the Christians. Read Polly's 'Find out' verses to see what the High Priest did.

But God was still looking after them. That night he sent an angel to let them out of the prison. The Christians were able to carry on telling people about Jesus.

This code will help you find the answer.

a	c	e	h	i	j
□	■	△	▲	▽	▼

l	n	p	r	s	t	u
✿	✓	✕	⊙	●	◗	◖

Prayer time

Lord God, thank you that you still love me and look after me, even when other people are horrible to me. Amen.

Christians believe that . . .

DAY 22 . . . God is great

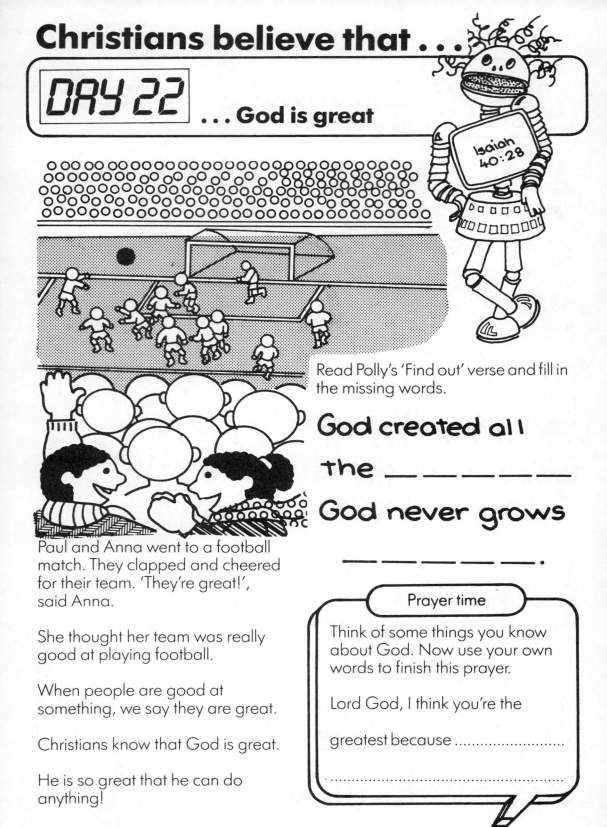

Isaiah 40:28

Read Polly's 'Find out' verse and fill in the missing words.

God created all

the _ _ _ _ _ _

God never grows

_ _ _ _ _ _ .

Paul and Anna went to a football match. They clapped and cheered for their team. 'They're great!', said Anna.

She thought her team was really good at playing football.

When people are good at something, we say they are great.

Christians know that God is great.

He is so great that he can do anything!

Prayer time

Think of some things you know about God. Now use your own words to finish this prayer.

Lord God, I think you're the

greatest because ....

....

Vicki made some clay beads at school.

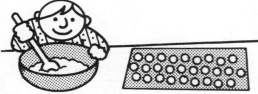

Peter made some peppermint creams.

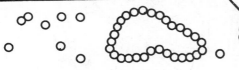

What do you like making?

....

It's fun to be able to make things.

But there are some things no human being could ever make. Draw a circle around them.

Colour the shapes with a dot in to show who made the things you circled.

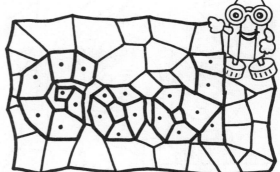

He made everything in our world.

Revelation 4:11

Prayer time

Read Polly's 'Find out' verse. Say it to God as your prayer.

DAY 24

Christians believe that . . .

. . . God's love lasts for ever

Psalm 89: 1, 2

Helen went to the fair with her uncle.

But God's love doesn't! Read Polly's 'Find out' verses.

Go by the sounds.

👁 🎀 bn t+ 🎩

your g 🧤

⛰ kw last 4 ever.

God never stops loving us. His love lasts for ever.

I wish we could stay here for ever.

Uncle Simon laughed. 'Everything has to come to an end, Helen.'

But Uncle Simon wasn't quite right.

Trips to the fair come to an end. Thunderstorms come to an end. Ice lollies come to an end.

Prayer time

Thank you, Father God, for loving me. I'm glad that your love will never end. Amen.

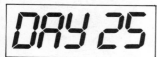

1 John 1:9

I'm sorry, Mum.

God has made us a promise. Read about it in Polly's 'Find out' verse.

When we do something wrong and tell God that we are sorry for it, he promises to:

☐ Tell us off

☐ Punish us

☐ Forgive us

Why do you think Alison needed to say sorry?

Mum knew that Alison really was sorry. So she said, 'I forgive you – but don't do it again.'

Prayer time

Father God, I know I do wrong things sometimes. Thank you that you will forgive me for them if I ask you to. Amen.

DAY 26

. . . Jesus is God's Son

Matthew 3:16, 17

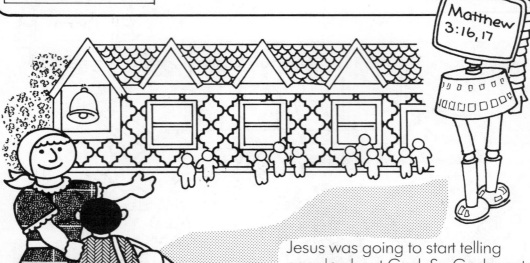

Jesus was going to start telling people about God. So God wanted everyone to know who Jesus was.

Ben was starting at a new school. On the first day, his mum took him along to meet his new teacher.

Read Polly's 'Find out' verses.

Join the dots to show what God said.

This is my son, Ben.

She wanted the teacher to know who Ben was.

Prayer time

Father God, thank you for your Son, Jesus. Amen.

DAY 27

Christians believe that . . .

. . . Jesus died and rose again

Matthew 28:5-7

When do we usually have these?

....

Easter usually comes at the end of March or beginning of April. Just before Easter, we remember that Jesus died on the cross.

It was God's plan for Jesus to die so that we could become God's friends. But God's plan didn't end there!

Read Polly's 'Find out' verses.

God brought Jesus back to life! What do you think the women said when they told Jesus's disciples the good news?

Prayer time

Dear God, thank you that Jesus is alive. Amen.

DAY 28

. . . Jesus is coming back

Acts 1:11

Can you work out the message Angela left for Karen?

Read Polly's 'Find out' verse. Then work out what the message was.

Nobody knows exactly when Jesus will come back. But when he does, everyone will be able to see him. It will be really exciting!

Use this code

a	b	c	d	e	h
●	□	■	△	▲	▽

i	j	k	l	m	n
▼	✓	✻	✿	+	∷

o	s	t	u	w	y
⊙	ɛ	▯	▮	▭	▬

Prayer time

Lord Jesus, it's exciting to think that one day I will see you. Help me to be ready to meet you. Amen.

After Jesus rose from the dead, he went back to heaven. But he left a special message for his friends.

DAY 29

Christians believe that . . .

. . . the Holy Spirit helps us

John 14:26

Draw lines to show who could help these people.

Help.

Ouch!

I'm lost.

So Jesus made a promise. Read Polly's 'Find out' verse.

Who will help Christians to keep following Jesus?

--- --- ---

--- --- ---

--- --- ---

Jesus knew that after he had gone back to heaven, Christians would need help to keep following him.

Prayer time

Lord Jesus, thank you for sending your helper the Holy Spirit. Thank you that he will help me to follow you. Amen.

Make a poster for your bedroom.

You will need:
some paper
coloured wax crayons
a black wax crayon
a paper clip

1 Colour the paper with the crayons. Use different colours and cover all the paper.

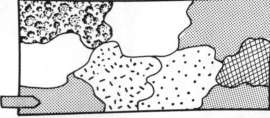

2 Cover over the colours with a thick black crayon.

3 Scratch some words on the poster using the end of the paper clip.

Here are some ideas.

God's love lasts

God is great

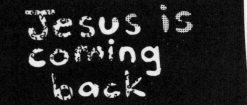

Jesus is coming back

DAY 30

Christians believe that . . .
. . . heaven will be great!

Matthew 22:2

Write in your name.

Buckingham Palace

Dear.................
You are invited to my son's wedding party.
Elizabeth R

Heaven will be much better than the best party you could imagine!

Use a mirror to see what the best part will be.

Jesus will be there!

If you were invited to a royal wedding, you'd certainly want to go. You would have a really good time there!

Jesus said that heaven will be like going to a royal wedding party.

Read Polly's 'Find out' verse.

Ask your mum or dad what they think heaven will be like. But remember — nobody really knows yet!

Prayer time

Lord Jesus, I'm looking forward to seeing you in heaven. With you there, heaven will be great! Amen.

More about Christians

DAY 31 — Jesus calls them friends

John 15:15

Write your name on this invitation.

Dear...............
I would like us to be friends.
Signed
The President of America

Read Polly's 'Find out' verse.

If the President of America asked you to be his friend, what would you think?

☐ It's a joke.

☐ I don't want to be his friend.

☐ Good. I'll invite him to tea.

☐ He must mean someone else.

☐ He's too important to be friends with me.

Jesus is much greater than the American President. But he calls Christians his friends!

Write your name on this invitation.

Dear........................
I would like us to be friends.
Love from Jesus

Prayer time

Lord Jesus, it's exciting to know that you want me to be your friend. Amen.

More about Christians
They get excited about the Good News

Romans 5:11

Rachel is excited about her good news. Use a mirror to see what it is.

I'm going to Australia to see my aunty Jean.

What is the Good News that Christians get excited about? Polly's 'Find out' verse will help you work it out.

G + zus

c m

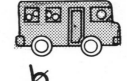

b

God's

Good news makes you feel excited inside!

Write or draw about some good news you have had.

Prayer time

Lord God, thank you for the Good News that Jesus makes us your friends. Amen.

John 20:30, 31

Fill in this file about yourself.

All about me.

My name is

My age is

My hair is

My eyes are

My favourite food is

My favourite colour is

My best friend is

Use a mirror to find out two more ways of learning about Jesus.

• talking to Jesus
• talking to other Christians about Jesus

People could read your file and find out about you.

How can Christians find out about Jesus? Polly's 'Find out' verse will help you think of one way.

....

....

Prayer time

Lord Jesus, please help me to learn more about you as I read the Bible. Amen.

More about Christians
They trust in God

I Corinthians 1:9

Katie was learning to swim. But she was scared of going under the water.

Don't worry! I'm here to look after you.

Write the first five words of Polly's verse here.

Katie knew she could trust her dad. He would stay near her and help her.

— — — — —

— — — — —

— — — — — .

God is always with us. He is always ready to help us when we ask him to. God will never let us down. That's why we can trust him.

Polly's 'Find out' verse has a special message about someone we can trust.

Prayer time

Father God, I'm glad I can trust you. I'm glad you will never let me down. Amen.

Make a musical instrument.

A tambourine

You will need:
a paper plate
some milk bottle tops

Attach the milk bottle tops to the edge of the plate.

paper plate

milk bottle tops

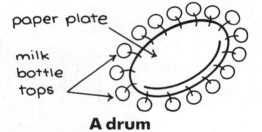

A drum

You will need:
a very large empty tin
a rubber inner tube
some string

Cut a circle out of the inner tube (make sure that it is larger than the tin). Stretch it over the tin and secure it with string.

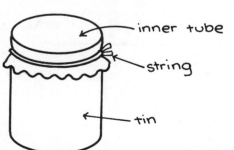

inner tube

string

tin

A shaker

You will need:
an empty plastic bottle
some rice, dried peas
or sand

Put the rice, peas or sand inside the bottle. Seal the top with sellotape or glue. Decorate the outside.

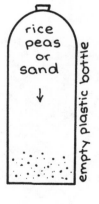

rice peas or sand

empty plastic bottle

You could take your instrument to Sunday school or church and play it when you sing songs to God.

Acts 5:29

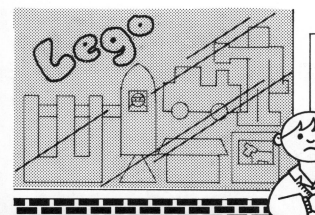

Chris was saving up to buy some more Lego. He only needed £2 more.

Dad's wallet was on the table. Nobody else was in the room.

Go on take it. No one will know.

God said you you must not take things that aren't yours.

It would have been very easy for Chris to take some money.

What do you think Chris did?

Sometimes it seems very easy to do wrong things. But read what Polly's 'Find out' verse says.

Christians try to obey God and do what he says, even when it is hard.

Prayer time

Use your own words when you see the dots.

Lord God, I find it hard to obey you when ....
Please help me to do what you want. Amen.

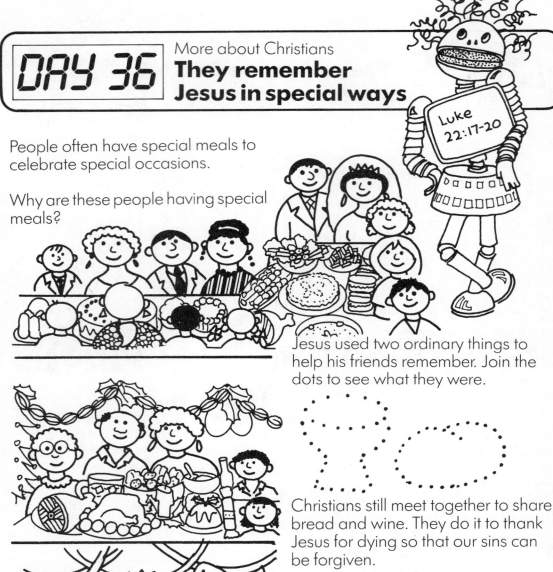

People often have special meals to celebrate special occasions.

Why are these people having special meals?

Jesus used two ordinary things to help his friends remember. Join the dots to see what they were.

Christians still meet together to share bread and wine. They do it to thank Jesus for dying so that our sins can be forgiven.

Find out how your church does this.

Jesus had a special meal with his friends. It would help them to remember why Jesus had to die. Read about it in Polly's 'Find out' verses.

Prayer time

Lord Jesus, thank you for giving us a special way to remember you. Amen.

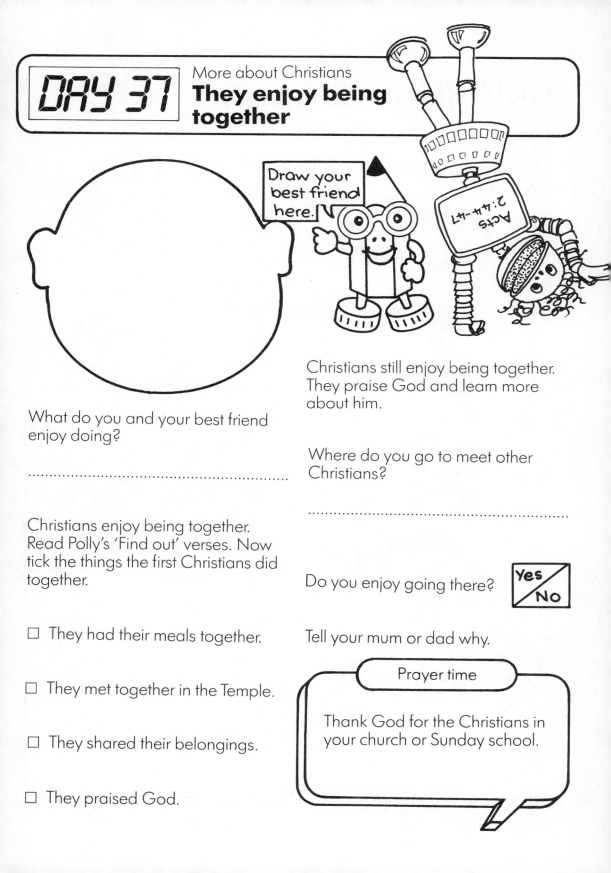

Draw your best friend here.

Acts 2:44-47

What do you and your best friend enjoy doing?

....

Christians enjoy being together. Read Polly's 'Find out' verses. Now tick the things the first Christians did together.

☐ They had their meals together.

☐ They met together in the Temple.

☐ They shared their belongings.

☐ They praised God.

Christians still enjoy being together. They praise God and learn more about him.

Where do you go to meet other Christians?

....

Do you enjoy going there? Yes / No

Tell your mum or dad why.

Prayer time

Thank God for the Christians in your church or Sunday school.

DAY 38

More about Christians
They sing for joy

Colossians
3:16

When you feel happy, what do you do?

☐ Laugh

☐ Clap your hands

☐ Hum

Christians are happy that they are Jesus's friends. It makes them want to:

☐ Skip

☐ Sing

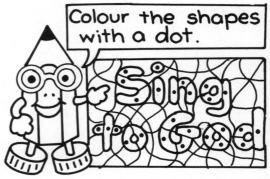

Colour the shapes with a dot.

Sing to God

Singing songs to God is one way of thanking him for being so great.

☐ Whistle

Anything else?...................................

Read Polly's 'Find out' verse.

Prayer time

Think of your favourite chorus or hymn. Sing it for God now.

 **DAY 39**

More about Christians
They tell others about Jesus

Acts 5:42

Simon had some news. He got a new bicycle for his birthday. He was very proud of it.

Christians have some news they want to tell people about. Read Polly's 'Find out' verse.

Write down the first letter of each object to see who the news is about.

Simon told all his friends at school the news about his bicycle. He couldn't stop talking about it! He even painted a picture of it!

Christians want to tell people the Good News that Jesus makes us God's friends.

Prayer time

Lord Jesus, please help Christians to keep on telling people about you. Amen.

Christians talk to God

He is always able to hear us

Mark 10:46-52

I can't hear if you all talk at once.

Katy's class were being very noisy. Her teacher found it hard to hear what they were all saying.

Jesus never finds it hard to hear us. No matter how many people are talking to him, he can still hear what each one is saying!

One day, Jesus was in the middle of a very noisy crowd. But he still managed to hear someone who was asking him for help. Polly's 'Find out' verses will tell you about it.

What was the man's name?

....

Prayer time

Lord, thank you that you always hear me when I talk to you. Today I want to tell you about .... Amen.

DAY 41

Christians talk to God
We can tell him when we are happy

Psalm 100:1,2

Jo-anne had a great time on holiday. When she got back she told her friends all about it.

Use a mirror to see what she said.

We went on an aeroplane. I saw an elephant. We went swimming in the sea.

Read Polly's 'Find out' verses.

We can tell God about the things that make us happy too.

Write or draw some of the things that make you happy.

It's fun to tell people about the things that make you happy. When you are happy or excited, who do you tell?

Tell God about something that makes you happy or excited. Or sing a happy song for him.

Prayer time

Tell Jesus about something that makes you happy or excited. Or sing a happy song for him.

Draw his/her face here.

DAY 42

Christians talk to God
We can tell him when we are sad

Matthew 8:5,6

Get the Roman officer to Jesus.

Why is this Roman officer sad? Read Polly's 'Find out' verses and tick the reason.

☐ His daughter had broken her arm.

☐ His servant was ill.

☐ His wife had died.

The Roman officer told Jesus why he was sad. Jesus helped him by making his servant better.

When we are sad, Jesus understands how we are feeling. We can tell him all about it.

Prayer time

Lord Jesus, thank you that I can talk to you when I am sad and upset. Amen.

DAY 43
Christians talk to God
We can tell him that we are sorry

Matthew 6:12

Tony has done something wrong. Follow the line to see what it was.

Tony punched Colin.

Tony told a lie about Colin.

Tony took Colin's sweets.

What does Tony need to say to Colin?

· ·

Sometimes we do wrong things. Then we need to tell God we are sorry for doing them.

In Polly's 'Find out' verse, Jesus tells us what we should say.

Go by the sounds.

4 + 💥g the ⚡r
🚌 ☀️💥d
🐝w have

Prayer time
Here is a prayer you could use to say sorry. Use your own words where you see the dots.
Father God, I am sorry that I

....

I know it was wrong. Please forgive me. Help me not to do it again. Amen.

Make a 'Thank you...' poster.

You will need:
a large sheet of paper
glue
scissors
magazines
crayons or felt tip pens

1 Write on the paper, 'Thank you, God, for . . .'.

2 Look through the magazines. Cut out pictures of things you could thank God for.

3 Arrange the pictures on your poster, then stick them down.

4 Put your poster in your bedroom. When you talk to God, thank him for some of the things on your poster.

DAY 44

Christians talk to God
We can tell him our secrets

I Peter 5:7

Can you guess what Kevin and Lucy's secrets are?

This code will help you.

a	b	c	d	e	f	g	h
□	■	△	▲	●	⊙	∧	∨

i	l	m	n	o	p	r	s	t	u
s	▭	▬	▯	▮	::	✳	✿	∩

Read Polly's 'Find out' verse.

Why can we trust God with our secrets?

Fill in the missing word.

Because God ___ ___ ___ ___ ___ for us.

Secrets are usually kept between you and someone you trust, like your best friend.

Prayer time

Lord God, I'm glad I can trust you with my secrets. Here's one that nobody else knows about

. . . .

. . . .

Christians talk to God
We can pray for other people

Jonathan's family went to visit his gran. His grandad died last year and gran sometimes feels lonely because she misses him.

When Jonathan got home, he decided to tell Jesus about his gran.

Dear Jesus, my gran misses my grandad. Please look after her and help her not to feel too lonely.

Read Polly's 'Find out' verses. The Jewish official told Jesus about someone who needed help. Who was it?

☐ His wife

☐ His daughter

☐ His gran

Prayer time

Tell Jesus about someone you know who needs his help.

DAY 46

We can tell him anything, anytime, anywhere

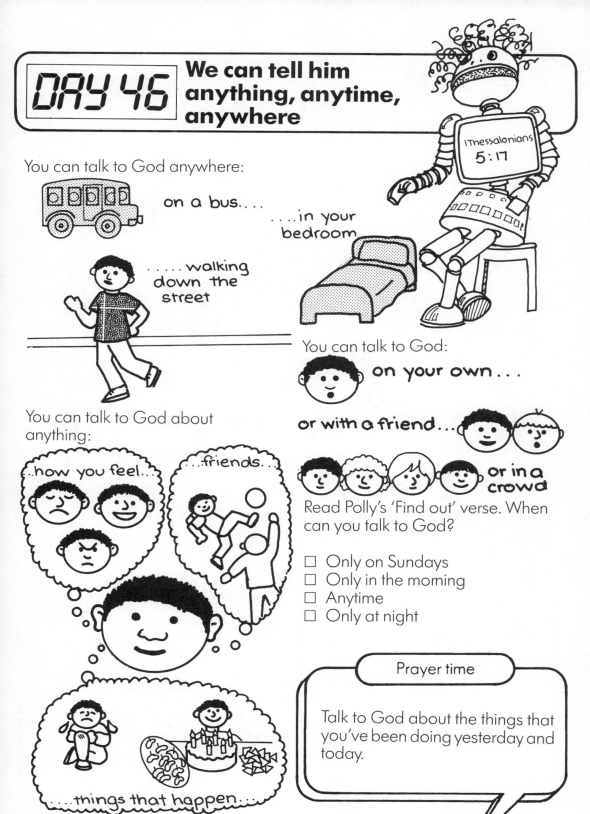

1 Thessalonians 5:17

You can talk to God anywhere:

on a bus....

....in your bedroom

.... walking down the street

You can talk to God about anything:

..how you feel...

...friends..

....things that happen....

You can talk to God:

on your own . . .

or with a friend...

or in a crowd

Read Polly's 'Find out' verse. When can you talk to God?

☐ Only on Sundays
☐ Only in the morning
☐ Anytime
☐ Only at night

Prayer time

Talk to God about the things that you've been doing yesterday and today.

Christians at work

A special job to do

Mark 16:15

Alison was given a special job at school. Her teacher explained carefully what she had to do.

Make sure you handle them carefully. When you have put in fresh water, give them a little bit of food.

Jesus has a special job for Christians to do. Use a mirror to read what it is.

Tell everyone about me

Can you guess what Alison's job is?

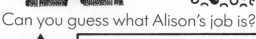

Write or draw about a special job you have at home or school.

Christians are glad that they can do this special job for Jesus.

Read Polly's 'Find out' verse. Which word means 'Good News'?

- - - - - - - -

Prayer time

Dear Lord, please help Christians to tell people the Good News about Jesus. Amen.

DAY 48

Sunday school leaders

Matthew 19: 13,14

Go away. Jesus is too busy for you.

Use these face shapes to draw some of your Sunday school leaders.

Who is saying this? Polly's 'Find out' verses will tell you.

The _ _ _ _ _ _ _ _ _ _

But they were wrong. Jesus is never too busy for children. He wants children to learn more about him, and he wants them to become his friends.

Sunday school leaders are working for Jesus. They help children like you to learn more about him.

Prayer time

Put your Sunday school leader's name in this prayer.
Lord God, thank you for

....

who helps me learn more about you. Please help him/her to have good ideas for our Sunday school. Amen.

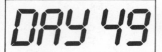

DAY 49

Christians at work
Church leaders

Matthew 28:19,20

What is your church called?

- -

Write down the name of your church's leader.

My church leader is ....
(You might also call him/her a minister, an elder or a vicar.)

Your church leader is working for Jesus. He/she helps the people in your church to learn more about Jesus.

Look at Polly's 'Find out' verses. What else does Jesus want your church leader to do?

☐ organise church outings

☐ baptise people

☐ sing well

☐ teach people to obey Jesus

☐ play the organ

☐ make people Jesus's disciples (followers)

Maybe your family could invite your church leader home for a meal. Then you could find out more about him/her.

Prayer time

Put your church leader's name in this prayer.
Lord God, thank you for ....

....
Please help him/her to lead our church well. Help him/her to teach us more about you. Amen.

Make a card.

You will need:
a piece of thin cardboard (about 24cms x 16 cms)
felt tip pens
some old magazines
scissors
glue

1 Fold the card in half.

2 Either: Draw a picture on the front of the card
or: Cut out some pictures from a magazine and paste them onto the front of the card.
Make sure that it looks really nice.

To
Mr. Smith
from
Sarah

Thank you
for
helping me
to learn about
Jesus.

3 Inside, write 'Thank you for helping me to learn about Jesus'.

4 Give the card to your Sunday school leader or church leader.

Galatians 6:2

Draw a picture of your favourite meal.

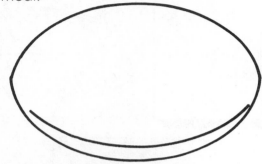

In our country we have plenty of food to eat. But in some countries, people do not have enough to eat. Maybe there wasn't enough rain to make the crops grow. Maybe there was too much rain. Maybe some people were greedy.

When a country does not have enough food, we say there is a famine.

The Christians who work for Tear Fund send money and people to places where they need help to grow more food. They are helping people, just like Polly's 'Find out' verse tells them to.

Find out some more about how Tear Fund helps other people.

Write to:
Terry Tearaway
Tear Fund
100 Church Road
Teddington
TW11 8QE

Send an extra stamp, so that Tear Fund can send you a reply.

Prayer time

Father God, thank you for my food. Help me not to waste it. Please help hungry people grow enough food to eat. Amen.

We hope you've enjoyed this 'Find out ...' book. Why don't you write and tell us what you liked best? Send your letters and pictures to Polly and Sam care of your national Scripture Union office. *(Send us an extra stamp so that we can write back to you.)*

Don't forget that there are more 'Find out' books for you to read.

Find Out about Jesus Find Out about Christians Find Out about God Find Out about God's Friends

Find Out about Bible People Find Out about God's World

When you have finished the 'Find out' series, keep on reading your Bible with Quest.

Quest has codes, puzzles, things to think about and things to pray about. It's great with the Bible!

Ask your national Scripture Union office for details of how to obtain Quest.